Discover The Anglo-Saxons

KINGS AND WARRIORS

Moira Butterfield

W

FRANKLIN WATTS
LONDON • SYDNEY

Franklin Watts
Published in Great Britain in 2016 by
The Watts Publishing Group

Copyright © The Watts Publishing Group 2014

Editor in chief: John C. Miles
Series editor: Sarah Ridley
Art director: Peter Scoulding
Series designer: John Christopher/White Design
Picture research: Diana Morris

Dewey number: 942
ISBN 978 1 4451 3327 0

Printed in China

MIX
Paper from
responsible sources
FSC
www.fsc.org
FSC® C104740

Franklin Watts
An imprint of
Hachette Children's Group
Part of The Watts Publishing Group
Carmelite House
50 Victoria Embankment
London EC4Y 0DZ

an Hachette UK company.
www.hachette.co.uk

www.franklinwatts.co.uk

CONTENTS

TAKEOVER!

In 410ce the Roman army left southern Britain for good. They had controlled it for 400 years, but now it lay at the mercy of new invaders who soon arrived by sea. The new peoples became known as the Anglo-Saxons.

WARRIORS ON THE WAVES

Bands of warriors sailed over from parts of what we now call Denmark, Germany and the Netherlands. They came in long wooden ships, each carrying around 30 to 40 men. Groups of three or four ships probably sailed over at a time, led by a war chief. At first these gangs raided the countryside and went home, but soon the visitors began to stay, taking over land and settling with their families.

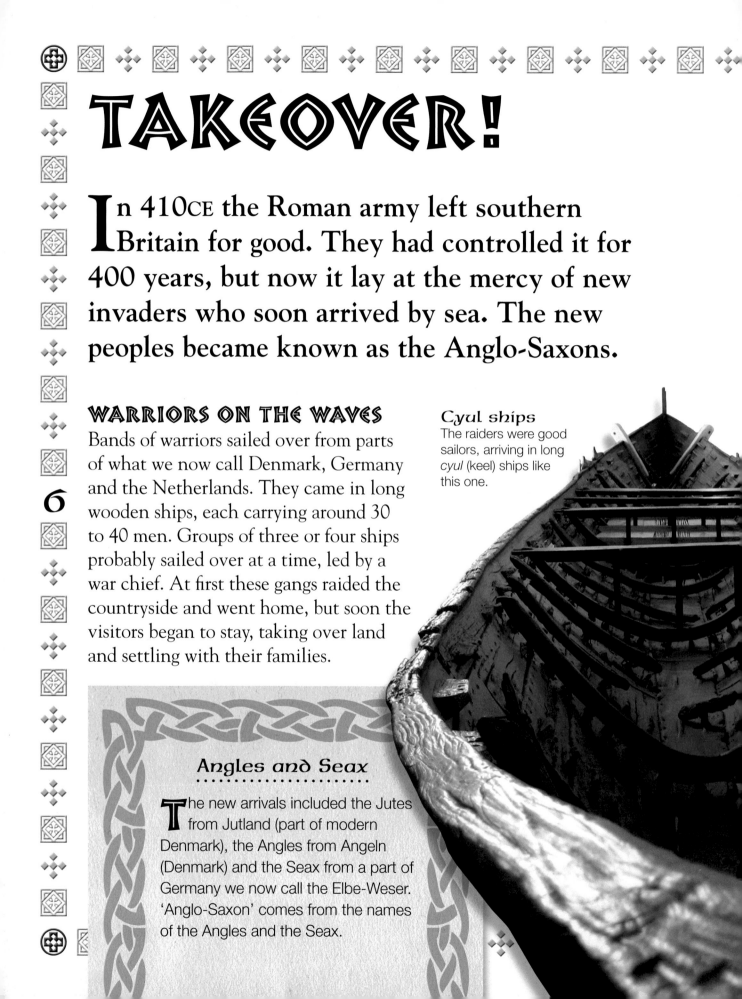

Cyul ships
The raiders were good sailors, arriving in long *cyul* (keel) ships like this one.

Angles and Seax

The new arrivals included the Jutes from Jutland (part of modern Denmark), the Angles from Angeln (Denmark) and the Seax from a part of Germany we now call the Elbe-Weser. 'Anglo-Saxon' comes from the names of the Angles and the Seax.

LEGENDS OF LOSS

Legend has it that in 449CE a local ruler called Vortigern invited a warlord called Hengist over from Jutland to help him fight his enemies. When Vortigern cheated Hengist, the warlord killed him, took over his kingdom and brought over lots more of his men. We don't know if this story is true, but later writings tell of local people being killed or made slaves by the new invaders.

Hot seat

A legend tells of local ruler Vortigern (above) being burnt to death in his fortress.

TERROR WRITTEN DOWN

A monk called Gildas who lived in the 500s wrote about what happened when the warrior bands arrived. He said that the local people were quickly overrun by the fierce invaders and that "the sword gleamed and the flames crackled around them on every side."

A LAND OF WARLORDS

In the 700s and 800s the south of Britain was split into seven Anglo-Saxon kingdoms – Mercia, Northumbria, East Anglia, Kent, Sussex, Essex and Wessex.

BAD NEIGHBOURS

Each kingdom had its own ruler. Nobody was king of all Britain yet. The local kings were a warlike bunch who continually fought their neighbours, trying to get more land and wealth. One of the most powerful rulers in the 700s was Offa, King of Mercia (centred on what we now call the Midlands). He built a dyke – an earth wall and ditch – to keep out his neighbours, the Welsh. It stretched for roughly 103 km along the edge of his kingdom.

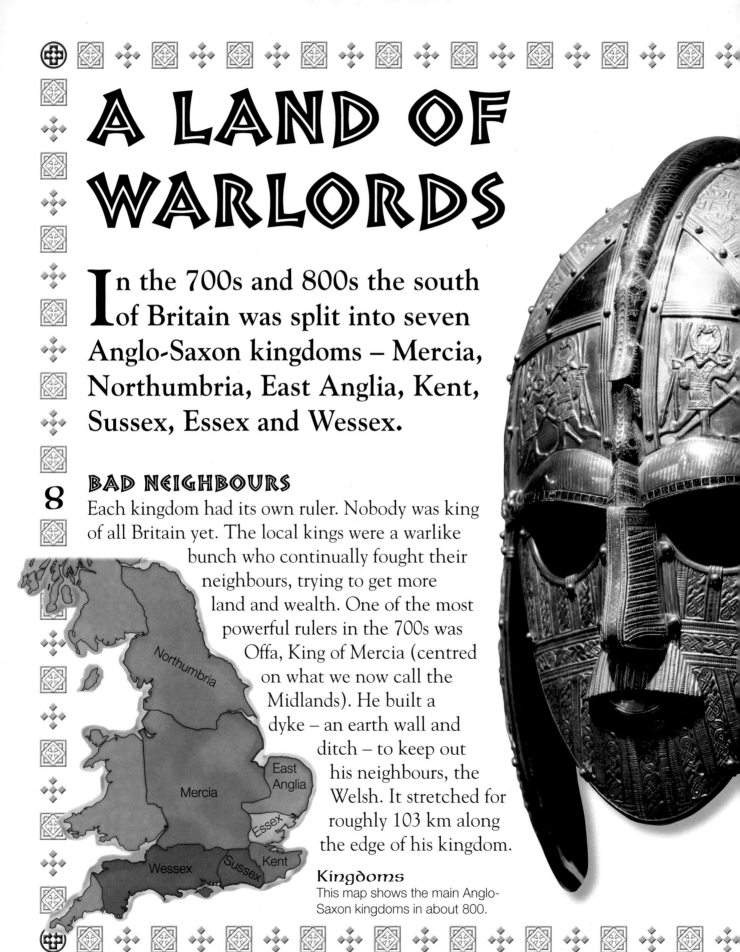

Northumbria

Mercia

East Anglia

Essex

Wessex

Sussex

Kent

Kingdoms
This map shows the main Anglo-Saxon kingdoms in about 800.

8

KINGS BECOME CHRISTIAN

When the Anglo-Saxons first arrived they were pagan, but in the 600s monks came over from other parts of Europe to convert them to Christianity. For a time they seemed to mix pagan and Christian beliefs together. Interesting evidence turned up when a mound thought to be the burial place of Redwald, King of East Anglia, was excavated at Sutton Hoo in Suffolk. In the 600s Redwald was given a pagan burial in a wooden ship, with treasures to take to a pagan afterlife. However, he also had silver spoons marked with the names of Christian saints.

Sutton Hoo helmet
Redwald was buried with treasures such as his helmet, decorated with pagan symbols. This is a reconstruction.

Top kings

It seems that some local Anglo-Saxon kings were more powerful than others, and had the title *bretwalda*, which means 'overlord'. In Anglo-Saxon writings King Redwald of East Anglia was called a bretwalda, but Offa was not. We don't know for sure what the title means. Perhaps the other kings chose the bretwalda to lead them in battle.

9

Redwald changes his mind

At the end of the 600s, an Anglo-Saxon monk called Bede described events from recent history. He wrote that Redwald converted to Christianity but was then persuaded by his wife to be a pagan as well.

THE KING'S CRACK FIGHTERS

The Anglo-Saxon leaders had their own bands of elite bodyguard warriors. The more successful a leader was, the more warriors he had. The warriors were prepared to fight to the death to defend their king.

Hall of the warriors

In 2012 the remains of an Anglo-Saxon feasting hall were discovered in Lyminge in Kent. The kings of Kent would probably have stayed here with their warriors. Among the remains were jewels, animal bones, a horse harness and a backgammon-style gaming piece. There would have been halls like this in all the different kingdoms of England.

TOUGH AND TRAINED

The king's warriors were called *housecarls*. The king fed and housed them in his hall – the base where he lived. He gave them wealth and rewards in return for their loyalty, and they had the best weapons and equipment that could be found. They were skilled at using their weapons, and though they fought on foot, they had horses for riding to and from battle. A grave from the late 500s, found in Lakenheath in Suffolk, contained a warrior with his weapons and shield and also his horse, sacrificed to go with him to the afterlife.

Fearsome on foot
Anglo-Saxon warrior bands fought each other on foot, as these re-enactors are doing.

FIGHTING TO THE DEATH

Loyalty was all-important between the housecarls and their king. They swore an oath to him, and were expected to die defending him on the battlefield. If a king died in a battle and one of his housecarls survived, that man was shamed for life. He might even be executed by his king's successor. In Anglo-Saxon stories, warriors are praised for their strength and bravery, but especially for their loyalty.

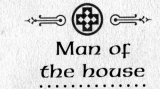

Man of the house

The word 'housecarl' comes from a Danish word meaning 'house man'. Together the housecarls were called the *hearth troop* – the troops who lived close to the king near his hearth (the fireplace in his home).

THE CALL-UP

A nglo-Saxon kings could call up extra fighters from local villages when they were needed. These local men made up a part-time army called the *fyrd*, rather like today's Territorial Army.

FYRDMEN NEEDED

In the Anglo-Saxon kingdoms there was a strict order in society. The king granted land to his nobles (*eoldermen*) and his lesser nobles (*thanes*). They, in turn, granted land to peasant farmers and craftsmen called *ceorls*. The land agreements that were made stated that, for every few acres of land, one man had to be sent to the fyrd when needed. He had to take his own weapons and horse.

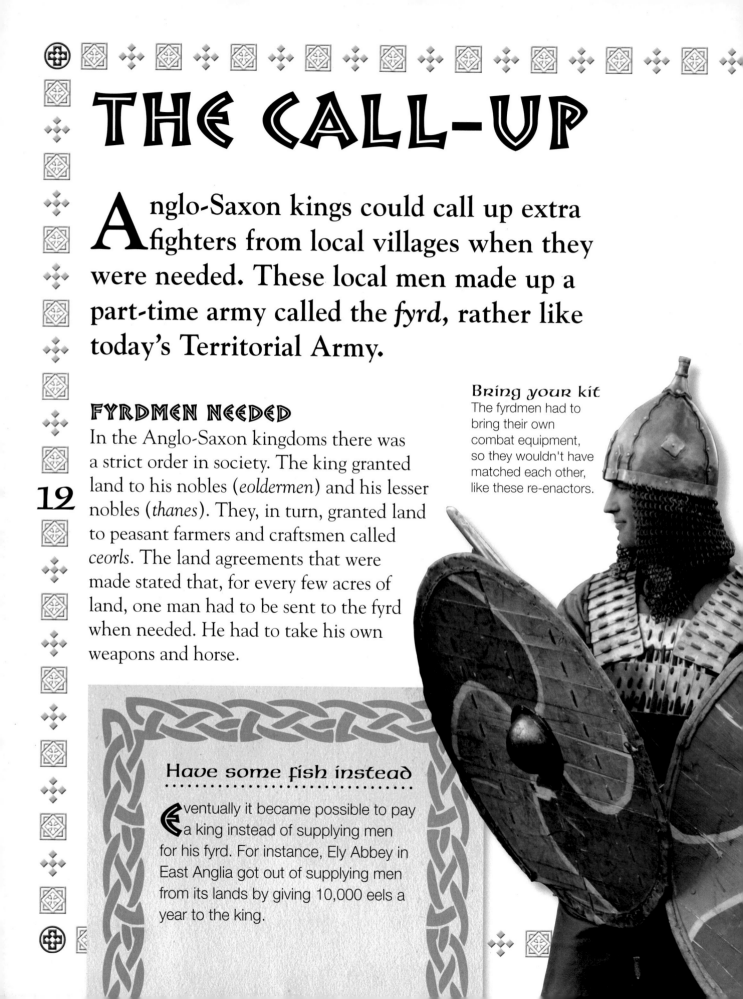

Bring your kit
The fyrdmen had to bring their own combat equipment, so they wouldn't have matched each other, like these re-enactors.

12

Have some fish instead

E ventually it became possible to pay a king instead of supplying men for his fyrd. For instance, Ely Abbey in East Anglia got out of supplying men from its lands by giving 10,000 eels a year to the king.

KEEP PRACTISING

The fyrdmen were probably experienced fighters. It's likely that they trained and practised their skills ready for when they were needed. They got some pay for joining the fyrd, but if they ran away in battle they forfeited their life and their lands. We don't know exactly how the fyrd worked, but it's thought the men might have been organised in small units, like a modern army.

Hide supplies

Anglo-Saxon land was divided into hides – a hide being enough land to support one family. Around one hundred hides made up a 'hundred', and each hundred had a leader responsible for supplying troops to the fyrd. The rule was usually one man for every five hides. Towns had to supply some fyrdmen, too.

ENEMIES FROM THE SEA

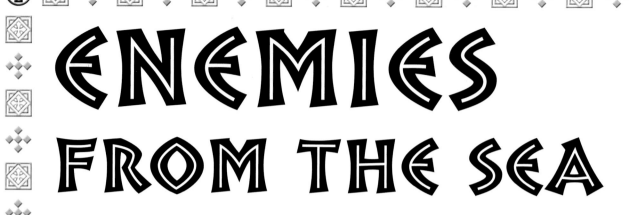

The various different kings of the Anglo-Saxon kingdoms fought among themselves until 793, when a new enemy from Scandinavia arrived to smash their world.

RUTHLESS RAIDERS

14

In 793, on a chilly January morning, a fleet of Danish Vikings attacked the monastery at Lindisfarne, off the coast of Northumbria. At first they came to steal. They grabbed Lindisfarne's treasures, captured monks to sell as slaves and sailed home. Viking raids similar to this grew more frequent until, in 865, a much bigger force arrived, nicknamed the Great Heathen Army. It set out to conquer land.

Grave events
This Lindisfarne gravestone depicts the Viking attack.

Scary ships
The Vikings sailed from Denmark, Norway and Sweden, using longships (shown right).

Violent times

A Viking saga (story poem) tells of a Viking leader called Ragnar Lodbrok being killed by the Anglo-Saxon King Alla of Northumbria in the mid-800s. Ragnar was thrown into a pit of snakes, but his son Ivar the Boneless took revenge by killing Alla using the Viking 'bloodeagle' method – sawing his ribs from his spine and then pulling his lungs out.

HARD YEARS OF FIGHTING

The Great Heathen Army landed in East Anglia, and for 14 years it rampaged across England. One by one the Anglo-Saxon kingdoms fell until only Wessex remained unconquered. The Vikings were pagan, like the early Anglo-Saxons had been. They lived by the same warrior code as the Anglo-Saxons, choosing their own war leaders and fighting for them to the death.

Cold camp

The Great Heathen Army did not fight in winter because it was hard to travel. Instead the Vikings set up camp. In 874 they camped at Repton in Derbyshire. Archaeologists have found Viking warriors buried there with their swords.

FIGHTBACK

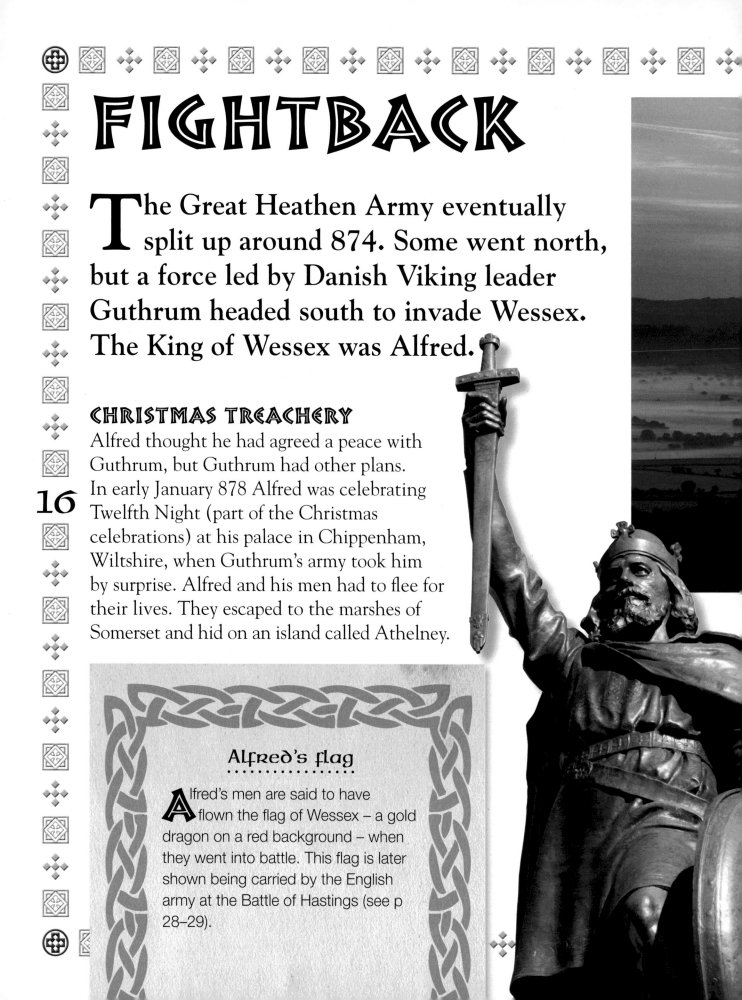

The Great Heathen Army eventually split up around 874. Some went north, but a force led by Danish Viking leader Guthrum headed south to invade Wessex. The King of Wessex was Alfred.

CHRISTMAS TREACHERY

Alfred thought he had agreed a peace with Guthrum, but Guthrum had other plans. In early January 878 Alfred was celebrating Twelfth Night (part of the Christmas celebrations) at his palace in Chippenham, Wiltshire, when Guthrum's army took him by surprise. Alfred and his men had to flee for their lives. They escaped to the marshes of Somerset and hid on an island called Athelney.

Alfred's flag

Alfred's men are said to have flown the flag of Wessex – a gold dragon on a red background – when they went into battle. This flag is later shown being carried by the English army at the Battle of Hastings (see p 28–29).

Alfred's hidden world

After his initial defeat, Alfred hid in the flooded marshes of the Somerset Levels, where only a few people knew secret routes to the Isle of Athelney.

THE FYRD TO THE RESCUE

When spring came, Alfred called his supporters together. He raised the fyrd – the men of Somerset, Hampshire, Wiltshire and Devon. They defeated the Vikings in a fierce battle at Ethandune, probably the village of Edington in Wiltshire. Then Alfred made the Vikings agree to a treaty whereby they would rule part of England, the Danelaw, and leave Alfred to rule the rest.

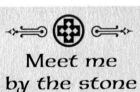
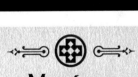

Meet me by the stone

According to Anglo-Saxon writings, the men of the fyrd met up at 'Egbert's Stone' to march with Alfred in the spring of 879. We don't know for sure where the stone was, but it was probably in Wiltshire, not far from Warminster.

FIGHTING, ANGLO-SAXON STYLE

The Anglo-Saxons rode towards a battle on horseback, but they fought on foot. They wore iron helmets and chainmail shirts, and carried spears, knives and shields. Some of the best warriors carried axes or swords.

18

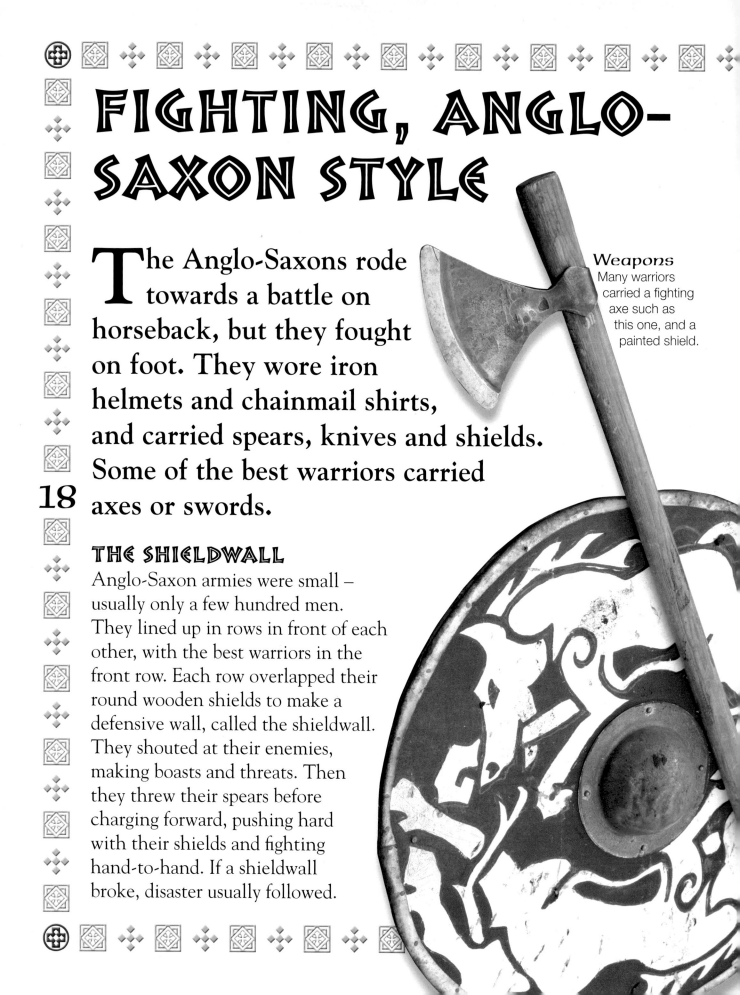

Weapons
Many warriors carried a fighting axe such as this one, and a painted shield.

THE SHIELDWALL

Anglo-Saxon armies were small – usually only a few hundred men. They lined up in rows in front of each other, with the best warriors in the front row. Each row overlapped their round wooden shields to make a defensive wall, called the shieldwall. They shouted at their enemies, making boasts and threats. Then they threw their spears before charging forward, pushing hard with their shields and fighting hand-to-hand. If a shieldwall broke, disaster usually followed.

Special swords

Swords were only for wealthy, important warriors. They were made of iron and took many hours of work by a skilled craftsman. They were greatly prized. Warriors gave their swords names, such as *aeco soeri*, meaning 'increaser of pain'! They were kept in finely-decorated scabbards (sword sheaths).

Luxury goods
Swords were very expensive, and only well-off nobles could afford them. Ordinary fyrdsmen were unlikely to have one.

Circle of death

The worst thing that could happen to a shieldwall was to be encircled by the enemy. Then the enemy could attack from all sides, picking off warriors.

A WEDGE OF VIKINGS

The Vikings used their own special tactic against Anglo-Saxon shieldwalls. They formed into a wedge shape, called the 'boar's snout', with the best warriors at the point of the triangle and the leader of the band in the middle. Then they charged, hoping that their weight and speed would drive a wedge through the shieldwall in front of them and make it collapse.

ALFRED THE BUILDER

Alfred had very nearly lost his kingdom, and he realised that if the Anglo-Saxons were to survive they had to re-organise how they fought the Vikings. He made important changes to keep them at bay.

20

READY AND WAITING

By the end of his reign in 899, Alfred had managed to take control of the whole of southern England. He did this by changing the way that he defended his kingdom. For instance, he realised that when the Vikings attacked, the fyrdmen were too slow to meet up. By the time they were ready to fight, their Viking enemies had already rampaged around the countryside, causing lots of damage. Alfred re-organised the fyrd so that half of it was always together, ready to fight straight away.

Alfred also built some longships – the first ever English navy ships – and took part in the first ever naval sea battle, in 882, against the Danes in the Stour Estuary in East Anglia. For this reason he is considered a key figure in naval history.

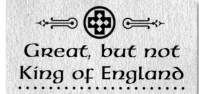

Great, but not King of England

When Alfred died he was not yet king of all England, but he had made the Anglo-Saxons a lot stronger and prevented a complete Viking takeover. He is seen as a hero of English history, and is the only leader to have 'the Great' put after his name.

The manuscript illustration contains Latin text:

Post uanis igitur magni cauda sed constituta e. qua fabule poetaru intastra ... nerua que primu ea excogitasse muium fuerat hominib: puiu habet autem stellas ... mo mali .iii. subcari ... na

stellaru ordinem nidius collocata dicant. ppt dicit. et mare qd antea nduali ingenio fecisse. ... in latere .v. in sum .v. sunt. xvii.

A reunis adla ... uda serpens plabitur argo.

Same ships

Alfred's ships probably looked rather like Viking ships. One of these is imagined in the manuscript illustration above.

STRONG TOWNS, STRONG KING

Alfred set up strongholds called *burhs* – towns with defensive walls and townsfolk ready and prepared to defend them. The burhs were scattered across Wessex, never more than 32km (20 miles) apart, so people from the surrounding countryside had a chance to flee behind the walls if the Vikings arrived. Alfred's capital, Winchester, was his biggest burh. Here he based his court and set about rewriting the laws of the land, to make the kingdom strong and well run.

Wessex walls

Alfred had walls or mounds and ditches built around his burhs. If there was an old Roman wall he built on top of it. In many towns today you can see remains of old walls that once protected the people inside. Some of the best examples today are Wallingford in Oxfordshire and at Wareham in Dorset.

FIGHTING LIKE FATHER

22

ETHELFLÆDA

When Alfred died in 899, his son Edward was chosen as King of Wessex. Alfred's daughter Aethelflaed became the leader of the Mercian kingdom after the death of her husband.

BROTHER AND SISTER OVERLORDS

Edward and Aethelflaed ruled different areas of England, but they worked together to push back the Vikings and reconquer more lands. They both fortified many towns to protect them from attack, and fought repeated battles with the Danes. Both were brave fighters. Aethelflaed herself went on many military expeditions and commanded her own warriors. Over the course of ten years the Anglo-Saxon forces gradually weakened the Danes, who eventually submitted to Edward or Aethelflaed as their overlords.

Fighting heroine
This Victorian stained glass window celebrates the memory of Aethelflaed.

Aethelflaed in front
This picture from the 1800s imagines
Aethelflaed leading her warriors against the Danes.

BROTHER TAKES OVER

Aethelflaed was called 'the Lady of the Mercians'.
She was hailed as a great leader and the Danes
of York had just decided to submit to her as
their ruler when she died, suddenly, in 918. The
Mercian nobles chose her daughter Aefwynn as
their new leader, but her uncle, Edward, had other
ideas. He persuaded them to choose him instead.
Aefwynn disappeared from history and Edward
became ruler of most of England.

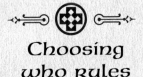

Choosing
who rules
. . . .

In the time of the
Anglo-Saxons, there
was no guarantee that
a king's child would
become leader if a king
died. The nobles had the
final decision, and would
choose the person whom
they thought would be
the strongest ruler.

FIRST KING OF ALL ENGLAND

Edward's son Athelstan was brought up in the court of his aunt, Aethelflaed. Her warriors taught him fighting skills and she taught him how to rule. When Edward died, Athelstan was chosen as King of Mercia and of Wessex, too.

24

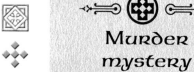

Murder mystery

Athelstan is suspected of murdering his brother Edwin. The story goes that he heard that Edwin was plotting against him, so he forced Edwin out to sea in a leaky ship, to his certain death. There is no proof of Athelstan's guilt, but it is true that there was some serious infighting between Alfred's relatives after the old ruler died.

THE BIG BATTLE

Athelstan was crowned in 925 and he claimed to be the overlord of all England. However in 937 he was challenged by a vast northern army of Scots, Irish, Welsh, Norwegians and Danes, who disagreed with his claim. Athelstan's Anglo-Saxon force met the enemy at the Battle of Brunanburh, thought to be somewhere in Lancashire.

The battle lasted for two days and resulted in thousands of deaths on both sides. Finally the Anglo-Saxons were victorious, and at last Athelstan could really call himself King of 'Engla-lond', the name for England at the time.

No mercy
The Battle of Brunanburh saw terrible slaughter. Luckily these re-enactors are only faking it!

WARRIOR POEMS

An Anglo-Saxon poem and an Icelandic saga were written about the Battle of Brunanburh. The poets talked about the great loss of life. One declared that never before had there been such a great slaughter of men on the island of Britain, and the battlefield was said to be covered in warriors' blood. Centuries later these Brunanburh war poems inspired J.R.R. Tolkien when he wrote battle scenes in his famous novel trilogy *The Lord of the Rings*.

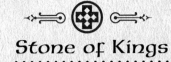

Stone of Kings

Athelstan was crowned King of Wessex and Mercia on the Coronation Stone at Kingston-upon-Thames. You can still see the stone standing in the town. Several Anglo-Saxon kings were probably crowned there.

ENGLAND GOES DANISH

Although the enemies of the Anglo-Saxons were badly defeated in 937, they did not give up. In 980 Vikings once more attacked, demanding money in return for peace.

LONDON BRIDGE FALLS DOWN

Ethelred II (the Unready) was King of England when the Danes arrived. At first he paid them money to go away, but they soon returned and set up camp in London. In 1014 Ethelred and his supporters rowed up the Thames to reclaim London from the enemy.

Unready for what?

Ethelred the Unready did not get his nickname because he was unprepared for trouble. In the Anglo-Saxon language 'unready' means badly advised. Ethelred may have got his nickname because he took poor advice or perhaps did not listen to advice at all.

According to legend, the Danish warriors lined up on London Bridge ready to throw their spears at Ethelred's incoming boats. Ethelred's men pulled thatched roofs off nearby houses to use as protection, then they tied cables around the bridge and pulled it down, tumbling the Danes into the river.

Although Ethelred won that day, two years later he had to flee. After his death his son Edmund Ironside agreed to share the kingdom with Danish King Cnut, but when Edmund himself was assassinated in 1016 Cnut became overall king. Cnut then strengthened his position by marrying Ethelred's widow, Queen Emma.

LAST STAND ON THE SHORE

A famous Anglo-Saxon poem, 'The Battle of Maldon', tells of a terrible battle defeat during the time of Ethelred the Unready. A local Anglo-Saxon leader called Brithnoth took his men to stop the Vikings invading the shores of Essex in 991. Brithnoth made the grave mistake of allowing his enemies to cross a causeway from the sea, and when fighting began he was soon killed. Some of Brithnoth's men ran away, but his housecarls fought bravely to the death around his body. Although the Vikings won, many of them lay dead, so the survivors returned to their boats and left.

Coin king
Coins showing King Cnut have been found in London.

27

Cnut connects
A Victorian statue of King Cnut, England's Danish ruler in Anglo-Saxon times.

England goes Scandinavian

Cnut also ruled Denmark and Norway, so for a while England became part of a Scandinavian empire. Cnut and his son ruled England until 1042, when Edward the Confessor, son of Ethelred the Unready, took the throne.

THE LAST BATTLE

Anglo-Saxon rule ended on 14 October, 1066. On that day, the Anglo-Saxon army, led by King Harold, was defeated by Duke William of Normandy and his invading troops.

KNIGHTS V. SHIELDWALL

Anglo-Saxon noble Harold Godwinson took the throne of England after the death of Edward the Confessor. Soon he faced an invasion in the north by the King of Norway. Harold marched north and won a great victory, but meanwhile Duke William of Normandy, a descendant of Vikings, had landed in the south. Harold had to rush his forces back to face William at Hastings in East Sussex.

Harold probably had between 7,000–8,000 men, including men of the fyrd and 3,000–4,000 housecarls. William had roughly 3,000 footsoldiers, 800 archers and 2,000 mounted knights who fought on horseback.

KNIGHTS WIN

Harold lined up his shieldwall on a ridge, facing the Normans below. All day the two sides fought, and for a while the Anglo-Saxons appeared to be winning, but at last the Normans broke down the shieldwall. Harold was killed and his housecarls stood around his body, fighting to the death.

Later accounts suggest that the Normans broke the Anglo-Saxon shieldwall by pretending to retreat. Some of the Anglo-Saxons saw this, broke ranks and ran after the Normans, who then turned to fight. We don't know this for sure, though.

Tapestry battle

This picture shows part of the 70-metre-long Bayeux Tapestry. Made in England, It was commissioned by the Normans to show their victory over the Anglo-Saxons.

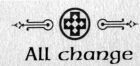

All change

Once the Normans triumphed, ways of fighting and of ruling the country changed. A new group of French-born nobles took charge. New ways of raising taxes were brought in and there was even a new language. Castles were built in England for the first time, and soldiers fought on horseback, no longer behind shieldwalls.

GLOSSARY

Angles People who arrive from Angeln (an area of Denmark).

Boar's snout A wedge-shaped formation of Viking warriors who charged at a line of Anglo-Saxons in battle, trying to scatter them.

Bretwalda The most powerful king in Anglo-Saxon England, overlord of the other kings.

Burh An Anglo-Saxon town with defensive walls and townsfolk ready and prepared to defend it.

Ceorl A peasant farmer or craftsman.

Cyul Long wooden ship that could carry 30 to 40 men.

Danegeld Ransom money paid by the Anglo-Saxons to the Vikings to make them go away.

Danelaw A part of England ruled by the Vikings in Anglo-Saxon times.

Dyke A long earth wall and ditch built to keep out neighbouring enemies.

Engla-lond An early name for England.

Eoldermen Important nobles.

Fyrd A part-time army of men called up by an Anglo-Saxon king when needed.

Great Heathen Army A big Viking army who arrived in 865 and rampaged across the country for fourteen years.

Hearth troop A king's bodyguard, who lived and fought with him.

Hide A measurement of land; enough land to support one farming family.

Housecarl A skilled warrior who acted as bodyguard to a king.

Hundred A measurement of land and a way of organising local people. Around a hundred hides made up a Hundred, and each Hundred had a leader.

30

ANGLO-SAXON TIMELINE

410CE The Roman army leaves Britain. In the years that follow local warlords take control of different areas.

449 The Angles and Saxons begin to arrive in southeast Britain. Local inhabitants fight to push them back.

540 The invading Angles, Saxons and Jutes conquer England. The monk Gildas writes about 'the Ruin of Britain'.

585 By now seven separate kingdoms have formed in England – Mercia, East Anglia, Northumberland, Essex, Wessex, Sussex and Kent. Each has their own Anglo-Saxon king.

Over time, some kings become bretwalda – overlords of the other kings.

597 Aethelberht, King of Kent, becomes the first Anglo-Saxon Christian leader, converted by the monk Augustine. Gradually others convert to Christianity.

620 (approx) The death and burial of East Anglian King Redwald at Sutton Hoo, Suffolk.

664 A meeting at Whitby decides between Celtic Christianity and the Christianity of Rome. The Christianity of Rome is preferred.

731 A monk called Bede finishes writing a history of Britain, the best source of history we have about this time.

757 Offa becomes King of Mercia. He builds a long defensive earth wall and ditch we call Offa's Dyke.

789 The first recorded Viking attack on the British Isles, at Portland in Dorset.

793 Vikings attack the monastery at Lindisfarne.

865 A big Viking force, the Great Heathen Army, arrives, and rampages across the country for the next 14 years.

878 Alfred, King of Wessex, defeats a Danish Viking force at the Battle of Edington, to save his kingdom. The Danes and the Anglo-Saxons agree to the Treaty of Wedmore, that

Jutes People who arrived from Jutland (part of modern Denmark).

Mercia Anglo-Saxon kingdom centred on what we now call the Midlands.

Normans People from Normandy in France.

Pagan Someone who worships many gods and goddesses, not the Christian god in the Bible.

Saga A long Scandinavian poem that tells an adventure story.

Saxon People who arrived from a part of Germany we call the Elbe-Weser.

Scabbard A long sheath for storing a sword.

Shieldwall A defensive line made by warriors standing next to each other, overlapping their shields.

Thane An Anglo-Saxon warrior.

Treaty of Wedmore A treaty agreed between the Vikings and Alfred of Wessex, splitting England between them.

Wessex Anglo-Saxon kingdom based in the southwest of England.

splits England between them. The word 'Englisc' is used to describe the people of Alfred's kingdom.

899 Alfred dies. He is succeeded as King of Wessex by his son, Edward.

911 Alfred's daughter Aethelflaed takes over the rule of Mercia after the death of her husband.

937 Athelstan, King of Wessex and Mercia, defeats an army of Vikings and Scots at the Battle of Brunanburh. He then rules over the whole of England.

1016 Danish King Cnut becomes King of England, deposing Ethelred the Unready.

Anglo-Danish kings rule England for a while.

1042 Edward, son of Ethelred the Unready, becomes king. He is known as Edward the Confessor. Brought up in Normandy, he apparently promised his throne to his great-nephew, William, when he died.

1066 Harold Godwinson is chosen as king but reigns for only ten months. The Anglo-Saxons are defeated by William, Duke of Normandy, at the Battle of Hastings.

WEBLINKS

Here are some websites with information about the Anglo-Saxons.

www.angelcynnreenactment society.org.uk
All about Anglo-Saxon fighting, written by re-enactors.

www.britishmuseum.org
Search for Anglo-Saxons on this giant site full of treasures.

www.regia.org/listings. php#weapons
Anglo-Saxon weapons and warriors.

www.royal.gov.uk
The official website of the British monarchy has a section on all the Anglo-Saxon kings. Search for 'History of the Monarchy', then 'KingsandQueensofEngland'.

www.battle1066.com
All about the Battle of Hastings in 1066.

www.show.me.uk/topicpage/ Anglo-Saxons.html
Anglo-Saxon themed games and online activities from museums around the country.

31

INDEX